Life:
THE PATHS AND CHOICES WE MAKE

LARRY REINHEARDT

Copyright © 2019 by Larry Reinheardt
All rights reserved. No part of this book may be reproduced, scanned, or distributed in any printed or electronic form without permission.
First Edition: September 2019
Printed in the United States of America
ISBN: 1645505359
ISBN: 9781645505358

Table of Contents

The Lord is My Sanctuary 1
The Miraculous Three Little Nails 2
God and the Atheist 4
A Letter to Mom 6
Let Go, Let God 8
The Soldier 10
My Peace I Give Thee 11
Where Do You Stand 13
A Vacuum in Our Soul 14
The Veteran 17
Peace with God 19
Awesome is Our Lord 21
The Warrior 23
The Search for My Lord 24
For The Love of God 26
The Forgotten War 29
A Price Was Paid 30
A Christmas Wish 32
Happy Easter 33
Hatred 34
My Partner, My Lover, My Friend, My Wife 35
Eyes That Cannot See Ears That Cannot Hear 36
A Dream of Hell 38
A Homeless Man 39
Guilty 41
By The Blood 42
I Have Eyes But Cannot See Ears But Cannot Hear 43

The Anchor	44
Hit Any Key To Continue	45
A Cry for Help	47
Life	49
Our Father in Heaven	51
The Change From Within	55

The Lord is My Sanctuary

There is a place I can always go
When I am troubled, lost and alone
It isn't a fortress of great stone walls
Yet withstood all the world has thrown

No army has ever been able to over run it
Though many an army has tried and failed
Though man has tried to stamp it out
Nothing man made has ever prevailed

You cannot see it standing anywhere
But it is there just the same
You have to take it on your faith
And know that it has a name

This place I go seeking sanctuary
Seeking peace in a storm tossed sea
My sanctuary is my Lord Jesus Christ
For He is always there for me

The Miraculous Three Little Nails

Did you know that Jesus Christ took three nails for you?
He did this not because he had to but because he loves you
He took your sins as his own though he was sinless himself
He did not whine or complain that it was not his sins
He was given the task to complete by God the Father
He knew what was going to happen to him and yet did as asked
Before the three nails were used to nail him to the cross he suffered
Humiliation of being punched, spit on, whipped, and crowned with thorns
And as the final step he carried his own cross to a place called Golgotha
They stripped him and spread him out on the cross for crucifixion
They used three nails to nail him to the cross to suffer and die
On that day he took on the whole weight of the world's sins
Because of the Father's love for us and by his grace we were saved
We have but to call on the name of Jesus Christ as the first step
Once we have called on him we must accept him as our Lord and Savior
By repenting, confessing our sins and asking forgiveness we are redeemed
You cannot earn redemption through any act you preform here on earth
It is a gift from God the Father and Jesus Christ because of their love

It all starts with the Lamb of God, three nails, and the precious blood spilled
It washed away our sins, it made Christ our redeemer, Lord, and Savior
If you believe in Christ and trust in him, he will stand before God as you advocate
Jesus stated in John 14:6 I am the way, and the truth, and the life No one comes to the Father except through me
So without Christ as your advocate you cannot see or go to the Father
Jesus Christ and three miraculous little nails can bring you eternal life
The offer is there, all you have to do is accept it, and it is free.
The choice is up to you, God loves you and is waiting with open arms

God and the Atheist

I had a dream the other night and it woke me with a start
God talking to an atheist who thought he was quiet smart

The atheist standing in front of God did not think this odd
I watched in fascination as the atheist deny there was a God

I stand before you in all my glory yet still you do resist
Why do you deny me when you can see that I exist?

I offered you salvation with the sacrifice of my only son
Yet you deny me still and the destruction that is yet to come

I know your heart and your soul for I gave them unto you
I also gave you free will to decide if my love is right for you

You know that I am really God or you would not deny me so
You listen to the world deny me and think this is the way to go

The atheist said Lord how could I believe when I can't see you
You can see me now yet you heart would still deny what is true

You must put your faith in me and trust my Holy Word as true
Your faith is trusting in things unseen and your life I will renewed

Still the atheist would not believe for of the world he would not let go

Being a man of this sinful world the Lord Father he would never know

And so as the father did walk away with love and a sadness filling his heart
For He had revealed himself to the atheist to offer him a brand new start

God had stood before the atheist and still he refused to change his ways
He could not let go of the sinful world or the sin that held him in sway

A Letter to Mom

Dear Mom,

How many tears have I caused you to shed
How many times have I broke your heart
You never said anything about the hurt
You were always there with an open heart

Did I really cause you all those gray hairs
Give you countless sleepless nights untold
I didn't realize how much trouble I was Momma
I'm sorry I didn't see I was making you grow old

Was I the cause of all the wrinkles on your face
Did I cause you to lose your beauty so fair
I know I wasn't the perfect child of which you dreamed
Far from it but yet you always showed you cared

How many prayers did you send to our Lord
Praying for me to mend my wayward life
And yet Momma you never gave up on me
Even though my sinful ways cut you like a knife

I know all your prayers you said for me did work
For the Lord has listened and heard your pleas
That which was lost has been found Momma
For the Lord does work and reside in me

You brought me back from the edge of disaster
You taught me to love the Lord as he loved you
It's never too late to show how loved you were
I doubt I ever told you enough the love felt for you

I wish I could see you one last time, Momma
To thank you for all the things you did for me
To tell you how sorry I am that I cause you pain
You are in my heart and will always be with me

I sit and write this letter to you, Momma
Though you are gone with the Lord to be
For I know you will get it still in heaven
For I trust in the Lord to get it to thee

Let Go, Let God

Our life hung by a thread in the early morning light
On the hill side were we choose to make our fight

We was young and afraid of the coming fight
But it was better in daylight then in dark of night

As soldiers we didn't know how this would end
Or if the outcome would be our lives to spend

But we know that we would give it our all
And we knew that we could quite possible fall

And as we waited on that hill with trembling heart
We lowered our heads in prayer before it did start

We prayed for help from our Almighty Lord God
Please see us through no matter what the odds

And as we sat waiting for an answer from God
The answer came to each of us Let Go, Let God

This fight is mine, I will see it through 'til the end
For I heard your cry to me for your brothers and friends

My strength is sufficient for you on this hill today
I have always been with you and never far away

As God lead us through with his guiding light
We left the hill that day at the end of that fight

And when ask by anyone how we found our way that day
We answered back "Let Go, Let God" for he is always the way

The Soldier

I have walked through the valley of the shadow of death
I have tasted the cold sting of fear as I went
I have seen the face of death up close and personal
I have went where others have feared to be sent

I ask for nothing form those that would give nothing
I have done what others would not do
I have accepted the loneliness of this life I lead
And should I fail I will accept that too

I have faced terror in this life that no one should have to face
And I have tasted the enjoyment of a sweet moment's love
I have ask nothing for myself but to give the best that I could
I have cried, pained, hoped, and prayed to God above

Most of all I have lived times that most say are best forgotten
It was never easy to live this life God choose for me
But I have tried my best to live this life He has given to me
And through it all he was at my side for he promised not to leave me

And when my race is finally ran and there is no more to say
Shed no tears for the life I choose and cry not at my grave
Just look back on my life and know that I ran it all the way
And remember me for what I was, "a Soldier" 'til my dying day

My Peace I Give Thee

I went to my Lord on bended knees for an answer to a pray
I found him in my room that day I had went to bend my knee
I told him I was searching for just a few moments of peace
His word came softly to me my peace I give to thee

I did not question why for his answer seem quite clear
He knew I was quite troubled and he was there for me
And like the father that he is, he sit and listen to my plea
His words came softly to me again my peace I give to thee

Lord I read your word from your Holy Book each and everyday
And as I read and study your word in my heart you plant a seed
But sometimes I don't understand your word and of't I go a stray
And yet again I hear his soft voice my peace I give to thee

For each and every trouble there is an answer for you to see
Continue to follow in my word share the love you have for me
For as you grow strong in my word others too that love will see
I will always be at your side child for my peace I give to thee

I knew he'd always be with me even though I couldn't see
For his word I held in my heart and my faith had set me free
As I knelt there with my lord a quiet peace fell over me
And my Lord spoke, you see child my peace I give to thee

There is no problem I cannot handle be it great or be it small
My Lord is with me, to help and guide when he hears my plea
So when I'm worry and in doubt I know he's listening to me
And I just remember the words he spoke my peace I give to thee

Where Do You Stand

What if tomorrow I were confronted with God, our Heavenly Father
What would I have to say to him when I'm suddenly face to face
Could I tell him that I stood up for him in the face of his enemies
Or did I just turn and run away in fear not leaving any a trace

Did I live as he asks me to live or just ignore his word completely
Would I be courageous when He asks me to lend a helping hand
And did I ask Him for the strength when this world tries to defeat me
Would I stand with Him in faith no matter when it came to make a stand

Was I ashamed of him when he needed me to show my faith
Did I deny his existent when faced with Satan's evil host
Or did I stand up against Satan thru it might cost me my life
And was I a warrior of the light to stand for the Lord of host

It is not easy when you find yourself with God face to face
You cannot hide from him what has happen in your life
The only thing that you can do is tell him all the truth
Put faith in Jesus promise that he is the way to life

A Vacuum in Our Soul

There is a vacuum inside each of us
There we do not like to go
It's like a large empty space
A deep dark empty hole

We try to fill it with worldly things
But always the hole's still there
For no matter what we fill it with
There's just one big vacuum there

We seem to think we can hide
It where no one will ever know
For come into the light it does
No matter where we go

Try as we might to hide it
Deep inside not wanting it seen
The vacuum is always there
For its where our God should be

For some odd reason we think
That God will not know or see
But God put that vacuum there
For it is his home to be

The only way we can fill it
Is to ask God into that hole

And once he fills that vacuum
Our soul becomes whole

He placed a soul in each one of us
Leaving that vacuum of a hole
And we must trust our God
He will fill the vacuum in our soul

He will never force us to accept him
But leaves that choice to us
And if we will allow his love in
He'll fill that vacuum in a rush

We have but to accept him
And he will reside within our soul
And oh the joy his presents bring
When he finally fills the hole

For his love and peace are special
And his love and peace we truly need
He will never leave nor forsake us
For he has said I am all you need

So if you have an empty hole
That inside your very soul
Don't try to fill it with worldly things
But ask God to make you whole

If we fill it with our heavenly father
He will fulfill all our need
And all we really have to do
Is ask and we shall receive

The Veteran

I am a Veteran of the United States Armed Forces
The life I lead was not easy and often filled with loneness
I was not forced to lead this life but choose it as my life
I accepted it and understood my service with its loneness

I am part of an elite fighting force that protects our nation's way of life
I serve my country proudly and if necessary will give my life for that freedom
As a Veteran, I understand this freedom is never free, there is a cost attached
I am willing to pay the cost like so many before me to maintain that freedom

I took an oath to protect this country against all enemies foreign and domestic
I will honor that oath and protect the United States with my very life if need be
My oath did not stop just because I finished my term of service and retired
And that oath will always be a part of my life which for a veteran it should be

I do not except anything in return not even a thank you for your service
I volunteered for and because of my love for my country and its way of life

I have found no other place on earth that gives you the ability to live free
And therefore I will stand up for the United States through any and all strife

If you threaten my family, my flag, or my United States be prepared for to fight
So before you start something in my country remember what it will cost you
As a Veteran of the United States Armed Forces I will fight and give no Quarter
I am a proud United States Armed Forces Veteran that will bring the fight to you

Peace with God

As we go through life we search for a relationship with our Heavenly Father
He asks that you bring everything to him in prayer and he will answer you
No matter where you are he's always waiting for you to call on his name
You just have to trust him completely knowing in his time he will answer you

We struggle through life trying to solve everything on our own only to fail
We only turn to our Heavenly Father after we fall flat on our proverbial face
We then expect him to pick us up and fix everything we have fouled up
And yes our Heavenly Father will fix everything leaving behind no trace

No matter how many time we fail he will be patiently waiting to help us
He is our Heavenly Father and his love for his children knows no end
He sent his only son to save us from our sinful ways so we might be with him
He did not have to send him but did it out of love for us to save us from our sin

It's time to stop searching for that relationship with our Heavenly Father above
So if you are still fighting our Heavenly Father though he wants only to save us
Stop the fighting and denying of our Heavenly Father who want only good for us
It's time to make peace with our Heavenly Father, God, returning the love to him

Thankful that he loved us so much that he was willing to sacrifice his own son for us
Be thankful and grateful that by this we received his saving grace and forgiveness
Commit your life to our Heavenly Father and his son Jesus Christ in thankfulness
Welcome him into your heart, depend on him, he knows that you need forgiveness

So step out of you comfort zone and away from your life so filled with sin
Go to a quiet room where you can be alone, get down on your knees and pray
Ask him to come into your heart there to reside and guide you through your life
Once you have ask him in and you make peace with him there he will always stay

Awesome is Our Lord

I knelt in silence at the edge of the trees
As I looked out over the morning break
I was searching for so many answers
For my heart and soul did truly ache

It has been a while since I had prayed
And to my Lord I did need to talk
Why is it Lord that I lose my way
And stray from your path I must walk

And as I knelt there on my knees
I prayed Oh Lord please come to me
I am in need of your wise counsel
Oh Lord I beg you to hear my plea

My child I'm here to fill your needs
You have but to talk to me
My love for you has not changed
Though you have oft' strayed from me

I know the questions you have for me
For I have known your life from the start
If you obey my laws and follow my ways
Home to me you come no more to be apart

And as I knelt there talking to my Lord
A sign did appear in the morning sky
For thru the trees I saw fiery cross
The Lord's wonder was set before my eyes

I know you will often stumble and fall
Do not worry for you have but to follow me
For through me you find life eternal
For that is as it was always meant to be

You have my word and my word is true
For I will never leave you all alone
I will stay with you both day and night
Until my child I finally bring you home

The Warrior

I am a warrior for our Lord Jesus Christ
I will defend him always both day and night
I have the Bible which is his Holy Word
I am the warrior who fights for the light

I will bring it to all that wish for the light
I am at war for those who are of night
I will give no quarter and ask for none back
For my life belongs to the Lord, it's for him I fight

I have willingly given my life to my Lord
I ask nothing of him but to honor his name
He is my strength and armor in whom I trust
And to his Holy Name I will never bring shame

I will fight the good fight as long as I breathe
Though in pain and suffering my body may be
And when at last I draw my final breath
Then shall my Lord Jesus Christ my eyes will see

The Search for My Lord

I walk these hills in search of the Lord
For I was lost and so afraid
I could not find him anywhere
For far from him I had truly strayed

I know He's here but the question's where
I looked in the woods behind every tree
I looked thru the valleys high and low
But I found him not oh where could my Lord be

The harder I searched the more lost I felt
For He did not answer my pleas
And He said He would always be there for me
Oh where oh where could my Lord be

And finally exhausted from my wandering search
I dropped down upon my knee
Oh Lord I've searched for you for so long
Why is it your face I cannot see?

Then the answer like a flash of light did flow thru me
It was right in front of me all the time if I but looked to see
I had been searching for him in all the wrong places
For I found my Lord in my heart just as he should always be

And now that I have found him, His peace does reside in me
He was never far away from me, it was I that could not see
My Lord does now reside in my heart with his love flowing free
He'll always welcome me home for my Lord has set me free

For The Love of God

What if for the love of God

We lived our lives just for God
We obeyed his everyword and commandment in the Bible
We prayed every day for his guidance and help in our lives
We then followed that guidance he gave it to us no questions asked

What if for the love of God

We instead of always being ready to fight against God and his Holy Word
We were ready to fight for God our Heavenly Father no matter when or where
We would be ready to stand up for him in the face of all enemies because he is God
And we would say Lord here I am what would you have me do for you this day

What if for the love of God

We took Jesus Christ at his word and took up our cross
We followed in his footsteps and were totally pleasing to God
We instead of only praying to him when we were in trouble or needed his help
We gave thanks to God praying and praising him no matter the circumstances

What if for the love of God

We stood forth and declared I am Christian in the service of our Lord Jesus Christ
We by showing our faith in our Lord Jesus Christ we could lead others to him
We did all things not to show others how good we are but to be totally please to God
We did all this because we really believed and loved our Lord Jesus Christ

What if for the love of God

We repented, ask forgiveness of our sinful way of life and thru his grace he granted it
We could show the world that our Heavenly Father is willing to forgive us of our sins
We by example could show the love our Heavenly Father has for us his children
We just accepted that God's love for us is limitless and has no boundaries or fences

What if for the love of God

We did all these things to be totally pleasing to our Heavenly Father and Jesus Christ

We did them not because we had to, but because we wanted to please God
We returned the love God has for us to him and put a smile on his face
We never strayed from him or left his side ever again no matter where life takes us

The Forgotten War

We were sent to fight in a foreign land
In a war that we did not understand
We were told it was necessary to protect our way of life
Though I often wonder why we were even in this strife
It made no sense why we were sent here
Leaving behind everything we held so dear
We saw there was no clear cut battle plan
Most often things got way out of hand
We fought in the cities, towns, and jungles
There was no front line it was all a jumble
All gave some and some gave all
But none refused to answer the call
And in the end, we finally lost that fight
For nothing was as simple as black and white
Most came home to ridicule and shame
From a war that left no one the same
Some still fight this forgotten war
For there is no way to truly close that door
For memories in their minds will not go away
They fight and struggle to this everyday
For those that lived and came back home
Remember the Lord will never let you go it alone
Though in their minds they are always MIA
And then there are those that are MIA
And for those that never came back home
Still we search in order to bring you home
For we do not forget our brothers we've lost
And we still try to find them no matter the cost

A Price Was Paid

A long time ago a price was paid for man. The price paid was of the highest cost. It was not a price where the individual had any choice about. There was no choice in the matter. From the beginning it was determined that this would be the cost. There was no bargaining, bartering, trading, or changing places or prices. There could be no maybe or indecision on the part of anyone concerned. It was set and there was no turning back from it. The one who was to pay the price was never asked if it was okay. He was given the task and told the price. He did not ask why he was chosen. He never said he would not pay the price. He never thought of himself at all and yet with the paying of the price he changed the course of history as we know it. Without this price being paid, would we even be here today? Would the human race have survived until now? I for one think not. The price had to be paid in order that we continue in our existence.

I have often wondered at the courage, strength, and will it took to know you are going to die in the most extreme pain and still sacrifice yourself anyway. I ask myself would I be willing to lay down my life for some strangers. I hope and pray the answer is yes. I should be no less willing to give up my life then my Lord and Savior was to give his life for me. My life became his to command when I accepted him into my life. He gave his life for me so that I might have my eternal life back. He died on the cross at Calvary so that all who believe in him and call on his name might live. To obey his commandments and laws should be an honor for all that are his people. It should bring honor and glory to him and his Father in heaven.

We live in a world today that is callous, corrupt, and indifferent. The United States use to be one nation under God, but we seem to have forgotten where all our blessings come from. We have taken God out of schools, out of our meetings, and now we have even taken him out of some of our churches. We can no longer display the Ten Commandments in our courts or schools. We have abortions, homosexuality, pornography and evolution being taught to our young as being acceptable. It seem we no longer fear God or the consequences of disobeying him. If we do not reverse this trend soon it may be too late for us all. We as God fearing people need to step up and say enough is enough. What has happen to "<u>God Bless America</u>"?

A Christmas Wish

At this time of the year it is so easy to forget why we are celebrating with the
commercialization of everything. We give and receive gifts and best wishes for a very
Merry Christmas. It is my sincere wish for you at this time of year that just for a moment
you stop and think of why this time of the year is so special to all of us. I don't know if it
is the actual date Jesus was born or not, but does it really matter. I think not. All that
really matters is that he was born, he lived, he died, and he came back to life to save
us. By this unselfish act we gained through him eternal life. So just for a moment stop,
give thanks, and celebrate his life. He gave so much for us even though we were
unworthy. Give thanks, praise, and glory To God and his son Jesus Christ for the
greatest gift of love that was ever given to all.

Happy Easter

What a gift we have received from God, our Father in heaven. At this time of the year we should stop and take a few moments to reflect on three special days. To those of us that are Christians these days have a very special meaning. These are the days that our Lord suffered and died for us. He suffered insults, whips, and a very painful death only to raise again as a living intermediary on our behalf before God. And in so doing sacrificed his body and blood to provide us with forgiveness for our sins past, present and future once and for all. But we should not be sadden by this event because it was God's plan to save us. John 3:16 tells us of how great God's love really is. Just listen to these words: For God so loved the world that he gave his only begotten son, that whosoever believeth in him shall not perish but have eternal life. Just think how awesome this is. Jesus Christ knowing what was to come, lay down his life willingly in order to be able to stand before God and say "Father, they have called to me, I have heard their cry, and their price has been paid". So while celebrating with the Easter bunny, candy, and hard boiled eggs, let's take a few moments to give thanks, praise and glory to God and his son Jesus Christ for this wonderful gift of love at Easter time. May God bless you and your Family on this Easter Holiday?

Hatred

Have you ever wondered why people or countries hate each other? Is it because they're different, or because of their skin color, or their language, or their customs, etc.?
If by chance you answered yes to one of these, you're wrong. Hatred comes not natural to man. He is not born with it. It is not hereditary. Hatred is a learned skill. It's taught to our children. They learn it at home, in the school, or wherever they might be. Did you ever wonder what would happen if all children ever heard, saw, and felt was love. Think of a world without war with everyone working and living together in peace and harmony with God as the leader. And believe it or not if this world is to survive that's what it will take, but after all that's just too much to ask. Yes, it's just too much to ask. And to think this idea is only 2000 years old. No one ever said love thy bother or neighbor as thyself before, or have they? Yes, there was one man who did, his name was Jesus Christ. And what did we do to show our love, why we nailed the man to a cross made of wood and let him die. Such outrageous ideas caused trouble and men like him were troublemakers to be gotten rid of quickly. So that was what was done. And 2000 years later we still have not learned the lesson. But someday we will if maybe it's not too late. Let us hope and pray to the Lord that it won't be. The piper will one day have to be paid.

My Partner, My Lover, My Friend, My Wife

There is a hole in my life where once there was someone
Gone now is that very special person with whom I was one
For so many years you were here by my side
You saw me strong and you saw me when I cried

You were my partner as we walked through life
You were my lover in the cool evening's light
You were my friend when I needed you near
You were my wife whom I always held dear

It seemed we first meet not so long ago
Then years went by and we both grew old
Together we thought we would have more time
But in this world we live in is not always kind

Gone now is the love I once had in my life
Home now to the Father has gone my wife
But held in my heart she will always be
Though no long will she walk near to me

Dedicated to my brother Alan at the loss of Lynn
His beloved wife.

Eyes That Cannot See Ears That Cannot Hear

I study from your Holy Bible for you gave your precious words to me
I have your word in front of me but yet it makes no sense to me
I look to see your face oh Lord, but my eyes they cannot see
My eyes are wide open but nothing can my eyes clearly see
I know you're there oh Lord through the words you left for me
What is it I am doing wrong oh Lord that your face I cannot see
I pray to you and read your Word yet nothing comes clear to me
And yet though my eyes are wide open still your face I cannot see

I talk to you oh Lord for you told me in prayer I must speak to thee
I cannot find you anywhere know matter how hard I listen for thee
I know youhear me Lord for your word tells me you'll speak to me
Yet as I am still and listen for your voice my ears do not hear thee
Oh Lord I ask what am I doing wrong that I cannot hear thee
What have I forgot to do oh Lord that you do not speak to me
I come seeking your voice approaching on bended knee
Let me hear your voice oh Lord, what it is you would have of me

The Lord did answer my question what is it you would have of me
He open my eyes that I might clearly see his face full of his love for me
He open my ears that I might hear in his voice the love he gave to me

He ask only that I believe in his love and with that love he set me free
No more is he lost to me in this worldly life full of sin and mistrust
For he has opened my eyes and ears and in his love I now fully trust
Gone is my anxiety, my fears and all worldly cares for which I did lust
For now I put all my life in my Lord Jesus Christ in whom I do trust

A Dream of Hell

I was awaken last night by a terrible dream
I was in a place with no sight nor sound
There was nothing there but a grayness
It was cold and gray with silence all round

I knew I was in Hell and all I could do is scream
For I knew that was some place I did not want to be
A place Lucifer and His fallen angels were sent
A place where the fallen who refused in God to believe

What if what we have been told all our life is all wrong
What if Hell is not fire and brimstone we've been lead to believe
What if Hell is the absent of God and everything about him
What if we had to spend an eternity alone never God to see

In my dream I saw Hell as a place of loneliness without God
An eternity of nothing but a cold gray emptiness without God's love
It was a place so empty that there is no sight, no light, no sound just silence
The constant desolation and separation from our Lord God and his love

For any believer in our Lord Jesus Christ and God his heavenly father
This would be truly be a place of Hell to spend eternity absent of God
With nothing but your own thoughts to keep you company in that absents
Knowing you can never go back and share heaven and the love of God

A Homeless Man

I saw a homeless man sitting by a church today
He held a sign in front of him quiet sadly
Upon the sign these words were written
My life was not always this way. May God bless you.
He ask for nothing, and yet his words had given much.
He looked like he had not bathed for a while
His clothes were filthy dirty, tattered and well worn
I stopped to talk to him and offer food
But mostly to ask about the words on his sign
He gave me no name and wouldn't say where he was from
His face was that of long suffering in a world gone wrong
There was a deep sorrow in his eyes that I had never before seen
His voice expressed a love that was not of this world
He spoke of God and the love God had for us.
How he had sent his only son to die for a world that didn't care or deserve the sacrifice
Yet his God was not angry because of this situation with his son
His God had planned for his son to come into world to save his people
For all that believe in his son and called upon this name there would be life eternal.
It was not something that could be earned but was freely given through God grace.
Yet we fail him constantly with our worldly concerns when he has told us to just let him for he knows our needs

And at that moment I was reminded of just how great God's love is for us.
And even if your homeless his love is still unmeasurable for you Thankfully he is true to his word that he will never leave you or forsake you.

Guilty

Oh Lord it's so hard to understand you've forgiven me
With all my failures I'm continuing to disappoint thee
And Lord I am so guilty at every turn I make
I fail to believe your promise you will not forsake
There is this small voice that does whisper in my ear
Reminds me I am a sinner and you'll not accept me near
It reminds me of my past life with all of my many mistakes
It reminds me I will never be perfect even for Jesus sake
I can't seem to make it go away and leave me be in peace
But mention Jesus name it does flee at the swiftest pace
Lord you told me I'm forgiven for all my faults and sins
And all I have to do Lord is follow you to finally win
It sounds so very simple if I just put my faith in you
But that voice keeps saying guilty, he will not have you
You say Lord, I must focus my heart and eyes on you
But Satan would have me believe that this is far from true
I know that I am weak with little strength of my will alone
But by submitting my life to you I've strength I've never known
And the little voice that bother me so much in everyway
Has fled so very far from me since you're in my heart to stay
I thank you Lord for helping me to find my way back to you
Now my life is in your hands to strengthen and see me thru

By The Blood

By the blood of Jesus Christ my sins are washed away
It does not mean that I will be perfect or that I will not stray
It means I made a choice to believe Jesus's words are true
The words are from the father and we know his words are true
I repented my sinful life ask forgiveness to start my life anew
By confessing my sin filled life he give me eternal life anew
And I do not have to stand before the father alone with my sins
Jesus is my advocate by the blood he shed to wash away my sins
His precious blood spilled out on the cross to set me free at last
As I stand before God's Holy throne I will not be brought to task
At the cost of Jesus life God's grace does set me free
No price that can be set nor could there any payment be
Only God's love of his children could pay such a high priced fee
Washed clean in the blood of Jesus Christ I submit on bended knee
No more a lost and sinful child for the face of Jesus I now truly see
Washed in his blood my sins forgiven my life with Jesus has begun
I will not be perfect he knows as I wait the coming of the son
Jesus is the King of Kings whom everyone shall face on a bended knee
And Jesus will be there at the final judgement to speak for you and me

I Have Eyes But Cannot See Ears But Cannot Hear

I study from you Holy Bible for you gave your precious words to me
I have your word in front of me oh Lord but, yet I still cannot see thee
I look to see your face oh Lord, but my eyes they could not see
My eyes are wide open but yet nothing can my eyes clearly see

I know you're there oh Lord through the words you left for me
What is it I am doing wrong oh Lord that your face I cannot see
I pray to you and read your Word yet nothing comes clear to me
Yet though my eyes are wide open still your face I cannot see

I talk to you oh Lord for you told me in prayer I must seek thee
I cannot find you anywhere know matter how hard I listen for thee
I know you hear me Lord for by your word you speak to me
Yet as I am still and listen for your voice my ears do not hear thee

Again, oh Lord I ask what am I doing wrong when I seek to hear thee
What have I forgot to do oh Lord that I cannot hear you speak to me
Open my ears so that I might hear your word as you speak it to me
And yet my ears are open but still I do not hear you speak to me

Let those who have eyes look and they will truly see thee
Let those who have ears hear for they will truly hear thee
Open my eyes and ears oh Lord for it is you that I truly seek
And as I sit there in your word it all became so clear to me

The Anchor

There is an anchor unto which I cling
For me there can be no other
It matters not how rough the storm
For steadfast it hold like no other

I need not see this anchor of mine
I just trust faith it will see me through
I place my faith in this anchor of mine
For it has always been steadfast and true

It does not bend nor does it break
For it is stronger than any steel
My anchor has saved me many times
It matters not what may be the deal

I have put my faith in this my anchor
And I trust the words be true
For my anchor is my Lord Jesus Christ
Who gave me a life brand new

He gave his life to save my soul
Ask only that I call upon his name
He gave forgiveness for all my sins
And he never once did he place blame

He ask me only to repent from life of sin
To cling to him as an anchor for my soul
So I now put my faith and trust in him
I cling to my anchor no more a lost soul

Hit Any Key To Continue

I SIT AND TYPED ON MY COMPUTER
OH! THE WORDS OF WISDOM I WROTE
BUT WHEN I TRY TO PRINT THEM OUT
MY COMPUTER JUST SEEM TO CHOKE

IT CHECKED MY SPELLING, MY PUNCUATION TOO
TO THESE WONDERS THERE WAS NO END
BUT TRY AS I MIGHT TO MY DISMAY
TO THE PRINTER IT WOULD NOT SEND

IT SEEM TO BE RUNNING ALONG JUST FINE
AND EACH WORD ON THE SCREEN IT RENEWED
BUT TRY PRINTING THE WORD THE SAME MESSAGE HEARD
HIT ANY KEY TO CONTINUE

FRUSTRATED AND MAD WITH THE COMPUTER I HAD
I WAS GOING TO THROW IT OUT THE WINDOW
BUT THEN DECIDE IF I MUST, I MUST
SO I HIT ANY KEY TO CONTINUE

A Cry for Help

I heard a cry in the cold dark night
Of someone given a terrible fright

The cry of anguish was clear and plain
It was as if someone was in unspeakable pain

This was not the path he would have chosen
But he could not abandon what words were spoken

It had brought him down on his knees crying
Asking why his soul inside of him was dying

He knew not what was the caused his pain
But know that he could not like this remain

He had lost his way through life's travels
And now everything in life begin to unravel

He looked for a choice another way
But choices came not for him this day

Finally it came to him what he must do
He cried out Lord Jesus help see me thru

While he kneel there pleading in prayer
He looked up to see Jesus standing there.

His pain and suffering all disappeared
His mind and soul were totally clear

Lost no more in the cold dark night
Lord Jesus with him and shined his light

I was that person who cried out in pain
I was lost in darkness until Lord Jesus came

He saved me that night so long ago
When my pain and anguish would not let go

Life

The Paths and Choices We Make

As we travel through life we are faced with many paths and choices. Sometime the path will divide and we have to make a choice as to which one we will follow. We will sometime pray, roll the dice, or flip a coin to make that choice. Most of these options are not the best way to make that choice. However we make the choice we have to live with the results. We can so easily lose our way if we are not careful.

I have live with the paths and choices I have made in life. Some were okay some not so good. Whichever it was good or bad you have to live with it. For the first half of my life I made some pretty bad choices and took some really bad paths. Thankfully I had people around me that never gave up on me. I finally found the Lord Jesus Christ and am at peace with myself. No I am not perfect and I still make my share of mistakes but I now know that no matter what happens I can go to the Lord and ask for forgiveness. He is always there and always listening. By my faith I trust in his word that he will never leave or forsake me. I don't feel I am qualified to tell you as an individual how to find him only refer you to his word which will be your guide. Prayer is always a good start. Talk to him as a person then listen.

I know in my heart that he give me this ability to write poetry as a gift. I didn't like English in school yet here I am writing. I have noticed that when I write that it calms me and opens me to his word. My writing is an outlet for me for all the choices I have made through life. I am not restricted to poems about religion but write a little something for everyone to enjoy. It is my hope that you find something in these writings that will help you when the path separates and a choice has to be made. The only advice I can give you is to keep your faith and focus of the light for it will be your guide on the path you should take.

Our Father in Heaven

Why is it we have such a hard time believing in our father in heaven?
We say we believe in him but our actions and words prove otherwise
Is the problem we can't see or touch him and must go on faith alone?
Or is it because we think we are smarter and thus much more wise

We cannot say we believe in him and not trust in his word
Going to church on Sunday saying we believe in you, Lord
But the rest of the week we do nothing but stray from him
He has a great love for us but we cannot have it both ways

Why is it only when we want him to do something for us that we pray?
Shouldn't we pray continuously to thank him, to praise and honor him?
The only time we seem to need him close to us is when we are in trouble
Then if he doesn't answer and give us what we want we get mad at him

It is strange by his word he has told us all we need to do is ask of him
He has said "that all things will be given to us if we but trust and pray to him
And when he does answer us with what we need from him are we grateful
Do we take the time to bend our knees giving thanks and praise to him?

He is our loving father and is always there for us with his arms wide open
His love for us is so great, he came into the world taking unto himself all our sins
He lay down his life for us not because he had to but because of his love for us
He made the ultimate sacrifice of his life so we could have eternal life with him

He said he will never leave us or forsake us even though we daily break his heart
Even though we fail him over and over again and fall short of the glory of God
Like a loving father he stands in the door way waiting for us to return to his side
By his grace and blood we are washed clean, forgiven of our sins before God

He made us in his image and knew our story long before we were ever born
He wrote it laying out the plans for our life with him knowing of our sinful ways
Why is it we are so disobedient and defiant of the love he offer to us
When will we learn that like a good father he wants only the best for us always?

There will come a time when we will have to face our father in heaven
As the Holy Father we'll answer to him for all our sins we have committed
We will have to explain all we have done in this life both good and bad
And he will sit in judgement of our lives deciding if to heaven we'll be admitted

When that day comes and we stand before the Almighty god for judgement
We had better have accepted the gift of our lord Jesus Christ as our savior
He is the bridge, the advocate, go between for us with our Almighty God
For without Jesus we have no hope of surviving the judgement of Almighty God

So why do we have a hard time accepting our Father's gift of our Lord Jesus Christ
It's through his love for us, he sent his only son to us so he could intercede for us
We have his word if we call on his name, repent and believe in our Lord Jesus Christ
We will be redeemed, saved when we stand before Almighty God to answer for our sins

There is no other way to be saved from the judgement of our loving father in heaven
No amount of good deeds, giving to charities, or anything else will deflect his judgement
Our Lord Jesus Christ stated it very plainly in John14:6 when talking to his disciples
"I am the way, the truth, and the life… No one come to the father except through me"

Our father has shown and given us the way to come to him through his son
It is the only way we will be received by our loving father in heaven
It must be through the grace of Jesus Christ the only son of our living God
He and our loving father will be in heaven to welcome us with open loving Arms

So the next time you are in church on Sunday think about this when you are sitting there
Is this what my loving father really wants and except from me as one of his children
Or does he want and except us to show our faith every day as an example to others
The answer is no for he said "Go out unto the world and bring the good news to others

The Change From Within

There comes a time in everyone's life
Where they are ask to make a change
There is no set time limit or schedule
But it will happen in time just the same

You don't recognize the need for change
For you've live your life submerged in sin
But there is that one small voice that cries out
And it come from your center deep within

Come to me my wayward son, come be saved
At first you ignore the voice putting it aside
You think it is nothing just a whisper on the wind
But it is always there and from it you cannot hide

You cover your ears and close your eyes
But still you hear the voice for it does beg and plead
I want only the best for you, why is it you cannot see
Why is it you ignore me and listen not to my pleas?

I require nothing of you but your acceptance
For which there is no cost or fee to thee
Change within you must if you are to accept me
It is my gift to you that will set your soul free

So when you hear that small tiny voice within
Know that what you hear does come from me
Know to that I've loved you from the beginning son
And this is only the beginning of a life that's sin free

As this change does happen to you
You'll draw closer and closer to me
Your heart will be a beacon to everyone
A light that will shine in the dark for all to see

And this change within what is it you ask
Why it your belief your faith that is finally free
It's putting your trust in a God not seen
It's God that causes this change to be

So when the change from within does come
Open your heart and set yourself free
Welcome God to change you deep inside
For God and Jesus his son are all you will ever need

www.ingramcontent.com/pod-product-compliance
Lightning Source LLC
Chambersburg PA
CBHW052118070526
44584CB00017B/2541